Spiritual
MAZES &
PUZZLES

Second Edition

SHELLY P. EMERSON

WESTBOW
PRESS®
A DIVISION OF THOMAS NELSON
& ZONDERVAN

This book is a work of non-fiction. Unless otherwise noted, the author and the publisher make no explicit guarantees as to the accuracy of the information contained in this book and in some cases, names of people and places have been altered to protect their privacy.

WestBow Press books may be ordered through booksellers or by contacting:

WestBow Press
A Division of Thomas Nelson & Zondervan
1663 Liberty Drive
Bloomington, IN 47403
www.westbowpress.com
844-714-3454

Because of the dynamic nature of the Internet, any web addresses or links contained in this book may have changed since publication and may no longer be valid. The views expressed in this work are solely those of the author and do not necessarily reflect the views of the publisher, and the publisher hereby disclaims any responsibility for them.

Any people depicted in stock imagery provided by Getty Images are models, and such images are being used for illustrative purposes only.
Certain stock imagery © Getty Images.

Scripture taken from the King James Version of the Bible.

ISBN: 978-1-6642-7283-5 (sc)
ISBN: 978-1-6642-7282-8 (e)

Print information available on the last page.

WestBow Press rev. date: 07/21/2022

Ten Commandment Maze

This Ten Commandment maze also contains a crossword puzzle. The commandments do not go straight through, they go in and out as it is part of life. You need to go through each of the 10 commandments to get to the end of the maze. Maze starts at the bottom right corner and ends at the top center, work your way up to where it ends. Find the words of the commandments as you are traveling through the maze. If you'd like to look deeper into the 10 commandments see the scriptures in the maze.

Fruit of the Spirit Bowl

© 2013 Shelly P. Emerson

Fruit of the Spirit bowl maze contains the names of the spirit. *The Fruit of the Spirit scripture: 22) But the fruit of the Spirit is love, joy, peace, longsuffering, Gentleness, goodness, faith, 23) Meekness, temperance, against such there is no law. Galatians 5:22 -23*

The maze begins at the banana at the top right corner of the bowl of fruit you need to go through each of the spirits to reach the end of the maze which is located at the bottom of the bowl. A little bit cross a word puzzle is in the maze as some spirits cross one another! Write the names of the Fruit of the Spirit below:

1) _____   5) _____

2) _____   6) _____

3) _____   7) _____

4) _____   8) _____

America's Maze

This America's Maze is of the United States of America and Mexico is a part of the maze. It begins on the left side above California and ends on the left side above where it started. You have the choice to go through America first then Mexico to get to the end or go through Mexico then America to reach the end.

© 2013 Shelly P. Emerson

We are living on Satan's Playground he is always playing around with everyone's life. That is why having a relationship with the Lord is important. This means wearing God's Armor! There is scripture you need to go through in order to get to the end. You can look up the scripture at any time. That will help you get stronger knowledge of God's Word and a closer relationship with Jesus. The maze begins in the middle of earth and ends on the upper right side of the ball.

© 2013 shelly P. Emerson

This Satan Out, Jesus In maze has the intention of knowing how kick Satan out of your heart and letting Jesus in. It begins in the center, on the left side of the heart and ends on the right side of the heart. You have to go all the way around the heart to get to the end. You cannot just jump the line. It has a few things you can do that will help you get Satan out; a few will help get Jesus in.

© 2013 shelly P. Emerson

This maze Jesus is Waiting at the Well has to do with the story of Jesus saving a woman who was covered with sin and was bound to hell. Jesus told her that what she needed was not in the well. It's the living water that she needed. That is what is needed for all those who drink the living water and will not thirst again. This story is in John 4:1-26. The maze begins at the bottom right corner and ends in the middle of the well.

This American History maze has to do with the history of the United States of America that we had faced in the past. It begins at the bottom left corner, ends above Florida in Georgia inside the outline of America and Mexico. You will need to go through: WWI, WWII, Civil Rights, Memorial Day, and Independence Day to reach the end located above Florida.

© shelly R Emerson 2017

This maze "*Living in This World*" has to do with living a life in this world, with Jesus in your heart. The maze begins in the heart at the bottom left corner. The end is at the upper right corner where it says Eternal Life. To get to the end you will need to go through scriptures and parts of Christian living in this world like believe, faith, obey, and trust; do not get trapped in worldly things.

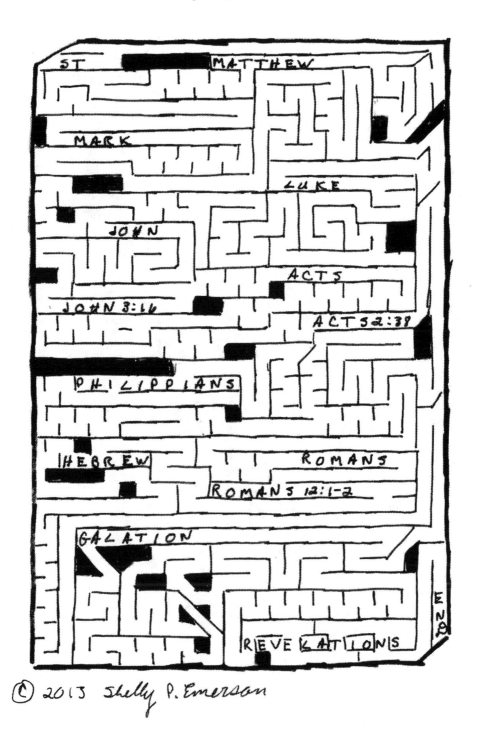

© 2013 Shelly P. Emerson

This is a New Testament Maze in the shape of a book God's Word. It begins at the top left corner as to the beginning of the New Testament. To get to the end of the maze located at the bottom right corner you need to go through 10 books of the New Testament. Revelations is the last book of the New Testament you have to go through the book of Revelations to get to the end.

Praying Hands

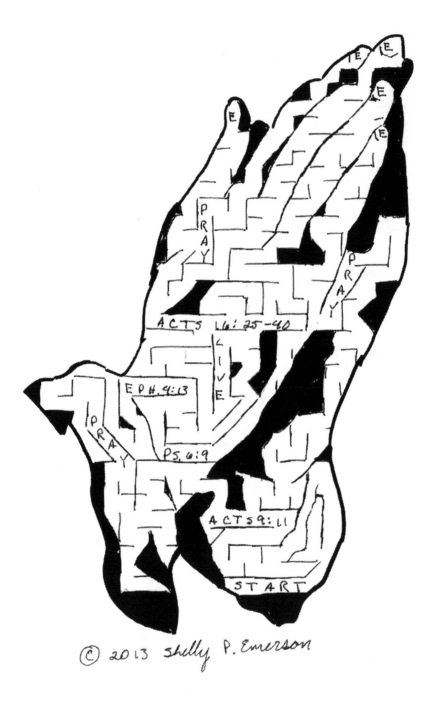

This Praying Hands maze has to do with discussing things of life with the Heavenly Father. God knows what our needs are before we have the words to ask He knows what the answer is to our prayers. He has perfect timing as to when and where the prayers are answered. This maze starts at the bottom of the left wrist. There are five endings in this maze because there being 5 fingers on one hand and prayer does not go out just one finger.

Crucifixion and Resurrection

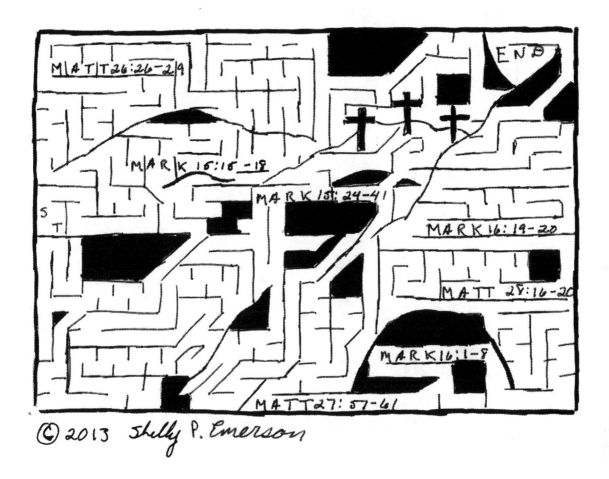

© 2013 Shelly P. Emerson

This Crucifixion and Resurrection maze is all about what Easter is and of the Last supper, beatings, the crucifixion, burial, the resurrection of Jesus Christ and His return to His Heavenly home. The maze starts in the middle on the left side and you must go through scripture to reach the end at the top right corner.

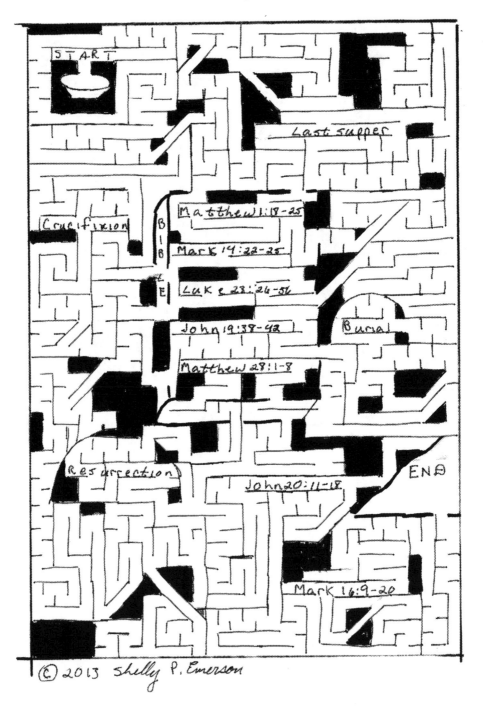

START

Last supper

Crucifixion

BIBLE

Matthew 1:18-25

Mark 14:22-25

Luke 23:26-56

John 19:38-42

Burial

Matthew 28:1-8

Resurrection

John 20:11-18

END

Mark 16:9-20

© 2013 Shelly P. Emerson

This Life of Jesus maze has to do with the birth of Jesus, last supper, the crucifixion, burial and His resurrection. The maze begins at the birth of Jesus lying in a manger in the upper left corner and ends near the bottom right corner when He spoke to his disciples. He showed the scar on His wounded hands to prove that He is alive; telling them He will return before left to prepare for us a place in his heavenly home.

New Testament Word Search

Matthew Mark, Luke, John, Acts, Romans, 1st Corinthians, 2nd Corinthians, Galatians Ephesians, Philippians, Colossians, 1st Thessalonians, 2nd Thessalonians, 1st Timothy, 2nd Timothy, Titus, Philemon, Hebrews, James, 1st Peter, 2nd Peter, 1st John, 2nd John, 3rd John, Jude, Revelations

D	J	A	M	E	S	J	M	C	J	D	Y	M	P	V	G	K	F	A	1	V	F	G
K	G	P	T	J	K	L	B	J	C	O	L	O	S	S	I	A	N	S	T	J	K	V
L	1	K	X	B	Z	Q	2	D	F	I	H	T	H	K	C	S	J	M	H	Z	E	A
N	C	G	D	D	K	M	P	J	C	F	M	N	Y	D	N	R	X	V	E	N	T	J
S	O	M	S	U	S	A	E	M	O	N	X	R	N	Y	S	O	M	J	S	C	O	V
B	R	T	L	U	B	T	T	A	N	H	B	V	S	T	A	M	E	R	S	E	F	Y
Y	I	K	T	G	Y	T	E	N	X	U	N	J	C	K	J	A	U	X	A	J	H	T
K	N	I	K	E	S	H	R	E	V	E	L	A	T	I	O	N	E	S	L	T	Y	S
P	T	S	F	M	D	E	J	D	P	C	C	U	L	S	X	S	X	J	O	A	P	Q
Y	H	E	B	R	E	W	X	B	J	H	N	E	K	N	R	U	I	M	N	S	S	O
N	I	I	F	1	V	U	M	K	Z	K	E	V	F	E	H	G	I	1	I	J	L	D
Z	A	B	L	T	S	B	V	S	A	R	T	S	K	S	V	T	P	J	A	C	2	M
C	N	K	R	I	J	K	K	O	H	I	S	H	I	K	2	E	D	A	N	M	C	L
B	S	S	V	M	P	R	D	I	K	Z	G	A	L	A	T	I	A	N	S	I	O	V
F	Q	B	W	O	D	I	O	R	V	N	J	Q	S	E	N	O	P	J	I	D	R	N
J	G	Y	O	T	B	K	A	H	N	V	Z	J	R	V	N	S	H	1	N	I	I	K
B	R	W	Q	H	J	M	L	N	D	R	V	A	B	H	Z	S	I	F	J	Q	N	V
E	J	J	B	Y	A	F	Y	H	S	H	N	M	O	K	B	M	L	H	F	O	T	Z
H	B	F	U	G	K	T	L	P	J	D	E	J	H	A	M	U	E	A	L	I	H	K
V	S	M	S	D	B	U	D	W	I	J	3	C	S	U	A	T	M	H	C	W	I	N
N	C	2	T	H	E	S	S	A	L	O	N	I	A	N	S	S	O	D	L	R	A	D
T	M	Y	A	C	L	W	L	E	M	F	J	R	K	R	Q	O	N	T	Q	J	N	K
X	R	D	U	Z	X	G	D	I	P	I	A	H	U	W	P	F	J	R	M	D	S	C

Know God's Word

© 2013 Shelly P. Emerson

This Know God's Word maze is to learn the reasons to attend church services. It begins at the bottom at the door of the church building and ends at the open book on the top of the church. At the start you go through either the right or the left hand door. The first and only scripture you will go through is Psalms 119:105. "Thy word is a lamp unto my feet and a light unto my path"

1) Why do we go to church?
2) What's the purpose of going to church?
3) What do we do when we attend to church services?

© Shelly P. Emerson 2017

This American Flag History maze is in honor of all men, women and counting dog veterans of the United States who are in the military to protect our country. The stars in this maze represent the military members of the Marines, Navy, and Army. The gray and white lines represent what the military does when putting their lives at risk. The maze begins at the bottom left corner and ends in the middle of the box of stars on the left. Side.

In God's Time

© Shelly P. Emerson 2077

This In God's Time maze speaks about things happening in God's Time. As to He has planned a time and place for things to happen in everyone's life. The scripture in this maze is about God's timing of when we have trials & trouble. The maze begins at the bottom left corner and ends at 12 O'clock on the clock in the center of the maze. To get to the end of the maze you will have to go through the scriptures scattered in the maze.

Paul and Silas

ACTS 16:39
ACTS 16:35-37
ACTS 16:27-30
ACTS 16:27
ACTS 16:31-34
ACTS 16:39-40
ACTS 16:25
ACTS 16:24

GO END

Paul & Silas

© 2013 Shelly P. Emerson

This Paul and Silas maze has to do with the story of when they were in prison. They showed their faith in God by praying and praising God even though they were chained in prison. Through the power in prayer God heard them and opened the door of the prison, broke their chains and set them free. This maze begins at the center bottom of the door and ends at the top right corner in the sun.

1) Who broke Paul & Silas's chains?
2) What did Paul and Silas do when they were in prison that showed the faith in God?

Christmas

MATTHEW 1:18-25
END
LUKE 2:14
MATTHEW 2:9
LUKE 2:12
LUKE 2:10
START

© 2013 Shelly P. Emerson

This Christmas maze has to do with the story of when the three wise men were told by an angel to follow the star which will lead them to the new born King. This has to do with the birth of Jesus Christ. The maze starts near the bottom left corner and ends below the golden star where Jesus was in the manger. You have to go through the scriptures listed in the maze to reach the end.

1) What is Christmas all about?
2) What did the wise men do?

The Woman at the Well

START

JOHN 4:10

END

JOHN 4:14

© 2013 shelly P. Emerson

The Woman at the Well maze is about the story of when Jesus was waiting at the well waiting for a woman who was covered with sin and was heading to hell. Jesus told her that what she needed is not in the well; it's the living water that she needed. That is what is needed for us all, those who drink the living water will not thirst again. This story is in John 4:1-26. The maze begins at the upper left corner of the shade of the well and ends in the middle in the center of the well.

1) What is in the well that we need?
2) What did Jesus say to this woman?
3) Is Jesus still waiting at the well?

Shield of Faith

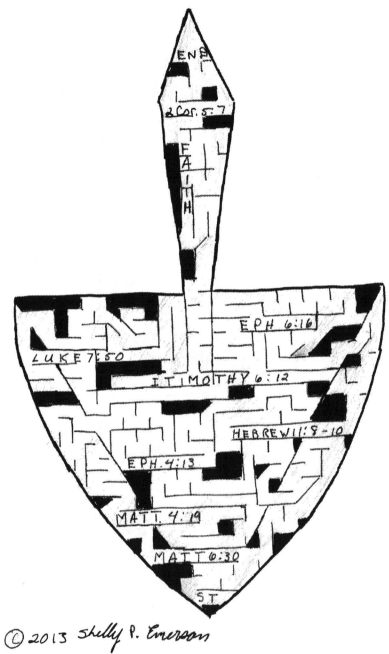

© 2013 Shelly P. Emerson

The Shield of Faith maze is speaking of two pieces of God's Armor the shield of Faith and sword of Hope. We as believers should wear God's armor at all times due to our battle we have with Satan, who is trying to stop us from following Jesus. The maze begins at the bottom of the shield and ends at the top of the sword. The scriptures listed are the steps for faith in Jesus. You must go through the scriptures to get to the end of the maze. If you desire to look deeper and learn more about faith and hope you are welcome to do so.

Old Testament Word Search

Genesis Exodus, Leviticus, Numbers, Deuteronomy, Joshua, Judges, Ruth, 1st Samuel, 2nd Samuel, 1st Kings, 2nd Kings, 1st Chronicles, 2nd Chronicles, Ezra, Nehemiah, Esther, Job, Psalms, Proverbs, Ecclesiastes, Song of Solomon, Isaiah, Jeremiah, Lamentations, Ezekiel, Daniel, Joel, Amos, Obadiah, Jonah, Micah, Nahum, Habakkuk, Zephaniah, Haggai, Zecharia, Malachi

Q	N	A	H	U	M	Y	L	V	X	F	Z	E	P	H	A	N	I	A	N	J	S	P	2	D
E	B	K	L	I	B	E	C	2	S	A	M	U	E	L	O	W	L	P	A	Z	Y	U	C	M
C	Z	N	T	L	I	Q	W	L	G	P	V	E	H	C	B	R	B	S	I	S	Y	B	H	W
C	G	R	R	N	B	J	H	J	N	E	H	E	M	I	A	H	G	E	S	T	H	E	R	B
L	H	M	A	N	R	U	O	P	M	E	U	H	O	V	D	X	Y	M	A	T	N	I	O	P
E	Y	D	W	I	N	D	R	B	Q	I	G	R	B	D	I	D	S	X	I	O	N	R	N	H
S	U	N	V	M	T	G	E	N	E	S	I	S	C	E	A	K	B	I	A	O	D	P	I	A
I	G	M	Y	W	V	E	L	Z	I	K	F	B	U	U	H	V	Y	E	H	B	S	L	C	B
A	2	K	I	N	G	S	K	A	M	O	S	N	D	T	J	W	H	Q	V	A	Y	E	L	A
S	P	Z	E	C	H	A	R	I	A	E	P	M	F	E	Y	A	D	X	L	E	D	V	E	K
T	F	L	B	Y	A	E	G	S	R	Y	D	I	F	R	N	P	W	M	Y	V	U	I	S	K
E	R	I	Z	B	T	H	R	E	I	N	E	E	X	O	D	U	S	T	X	Z	T	T	J	U
S	E	Z	E	K	I	E	L	Q	D	W	T	Y	J	N	E	G	U	E	G	A	V	I	A	K
Q	V	Y	S	I	B	Z	V	L	T	1	C	H	R	O	N	I	C	L	E	S	I	C	P	B
M	Z	G	A	M	A	U	W	E	N	C	E	J	N	M	K	X	H	M	T	S	B	U	R	A
Q	V	R	U	T	H	G	J	U	R	P	O	Z	E	Y	K	Y	1	K	I	N	G	S	N	T
D	A	N	G	F	C	V	G	M	W	E	T	C	M	R	U	E	H	C	A	Z	S	C	D	W
B	X	C	V	D	G	Z	B	A	L	G	C	A	G	V	E	T	N	J	X	B	M	C	S	G
H	Q	V	F	H	S	J	O	S	H	U	A	C	B	A	M	M	N	R	V	N	S	G	E	F
M	V	J	Z	N	J	F	D	1	M	A	L	A	C	H	I	V	I	F	H	C	N	R	C	Y
V	P	R	O	V	E	R	B	S	B	M	S	L	A	M	E	N	T	A	T	I	O	N	S	B
T	K	V	U	L	S	O	N	G	O	F	S	O	L	O	M	O	N	W	H	N	T	E	J	Y

God's Royal Kingdom

© Shelly R. Emerson 2017

God's Royal Kingdom maze shows the way to Heaven; there is only one way to God's Kingdom. It begins at the bottom right corner and the choice is yours to end at either: Satan's Evil Kingdom, God's Royal Kingdom, or this World. Going through the steps of salvation is the only way to reach God's Kingdom., located at the top between Satan's Evil kingdom and this world.

Three Starts One Ending

© 2013 shelly P. Emerson

This Three Starts One Ending maze is about Satan always using excuses to stop and pull people away from going to church to learn God's Word, worship, and praise the Lord for what He has done for us. You have a choice of where you want to, start one is near the upper left corner, start two is close to the lower middle right corner and start three is located near the bottom left corner The end of the maze is at the door of the church in the middle of the maze there are a few traps you will need to watch out for!

Bible Word Search

Old Testament: Genesis, Exodus, Leviticus, Numbers, Deuteronomy, Joshua, Judges, Ruth, 1 Samuel, 2 Samuel, 1 Kings, 2 Kings, 1 Chronicles, 2 Chronicles, Ezra, Nehemiah, Esther Job, Psalms, Proverbs, Ecclesiastes, Song of Solomon, Isaiah, Jeremiah, Lamentations, Ezekiel, Daniel, Joel, Amos, Obadiah, Jonah, Micah, Nahum, Habakkuk, Zephaniah, Haggai, Zecharia, Malachi

New Testament: Matthew, Mark, Luke, John, Acts, Romans, 1 Corinthians, 2 Corinthians, Galatians, Ephesians, Philippians, Colossians, 1 Thessalonians, 2 Thessalonians, 1 Timothy, 2 Timothy, Titus, Philemon, Hebrews, James, 1 Peter, 2 Peter, 1 John 2 John, 3 John, Jude, Revelations

F	L	H	2	T	H	E	S	S	A	L	O	N	I	A	N	S	D	A	N	I	E	L	M
P	S	A	D	Q	1	J	O	H	N	P	J	Y	E	P	D	1	P	E	T	E	R	A	I
O	O	B	M	L	K	F	V	H	E	E	T	D	U	F	R	T	J	O	B	O	T	L	C
B	N	A	G	E	I	U	O	A	G	B	Z	C	B	J	I	O	Y	O	M	T	J	E	A
A	G	K	Y	I	N	H	Y	C	A	N	R	R	O	V	E	T	V	A	H	P	U	V	H
D	O	K	1	I	G	Y	F	I	L	S	K	E	A	L	X	B	N	E	J	N	D	I	Z
I	F	U	C	L	S	N	A	M	A	J	N	A	W	F	O	S	W	B	R	T	E	T	E
A	S	K	H	M	P	Y	H	T	T	K	A	A	T	S	D	S	H	J	O	B	G	I	C
H	O	G	R	H	A	G	G	A	I	F	J	M	I	V	U	N	S	S	O	R	S	C	H
P	L	T	O	L	F	R	X	U	O	O	V	S	E	N	S	Q	2	I	Z	S	C	U	A
M	O	F	N	X	G	Z	K	C	N	B	N	X	S	S	O	Y	W	J	A	L	H	S	R
C	M	2	I	J	U	D	G	E	S	D	X	S	P	H	I	L	E	M	O	N	J	U	I
V	O	S	C	E	C	C	L	E	S	I	A	S	T	E	S	K	A	1	P	H	S	W	A
F	N	A	A	O	R	E	V	E	L	A	T	I	O	N	S	L	V	S	Y	E	N	Y	J
X	E	M	L	B	R	F	E	M	Y	Y	N	S	G	X	G	U	Z	A	S	N	G	O	R
P	H	U	S	D	N	I	I	Z	H	J	M	G	L	P	J	E	G	M	O	E	N	I	3
Q	R	E	S	N	I	P	T	T	E	N	B	O	H	A	X	W	N	U	N	A	H	J	Z
Y	E	L	G	B	U	J	O	H	N	K	A	J	N	E	C	D	E	E	H	T	O	T	F
O	H	F	N	E	T	M	W	O	I	F	I	H	Y	O	M	I	S	L	S	H	D	J	1
I	T	P	I	P	I	L	B	H	R	A	Y	E	U	I	R	I	N	F	N	I	O	R	T
H	S	X	K	T	T	U	G	E	Q	C	N	P	L	M	S	E	A	O	C	N	S	E	I
C	E	G	2	S	U	K	U	E	R	T	H	S	D	Y	R	A	T	H	R	T	H	T	M
A	A	M	O	S	S	E	P	H	E	S	I	A	N	S	V	I	I	U	M	H	F	E	O
L	Z	E	P	H	A	N	I	A	H	S	P	L	G	C	T	B	T	A	E	A	C	P	T
A	1	C	O	R	I	T	H	I	A	N	S	M	S	U	K	H	G	N	H	D	T	2	H
M	P	H	I	L	L	I	P	P	I	A	N	S	S	J	E	R	E	M	I	A	H	H	Y

Fruit of the Spirit Tree

© 2013 Shelly P. Emerson

But the fruit of the Spirit is love, joy, peace, longsuffering, Gentleness, goodness, faith, Meekness, temperance, against such there is no law. Galatians 5:22 -23

The Fruit of the Spirit Tree maze contains the names of the spirit. It begins at the bottom left corner. You will need to go through each one of the branches; in addition, some of the branches have one or two of their own. The ends of the maze is located at the top right corner in the sun

What Would Jesus Do?

© Shelly P. Emerson 2017

This "What Would Jesus Do?" maze is a question you should ask yourself daily while going through life. For example, what would Jesus do for a homeless person? There are a few traps in this maze, and they are things that Jesus would not do. The maze begins at the center bottom when you start, you choose to go either left or right. The end is at the top right corner.

Fruit of the Spirit Branches

© shelly P. Emerson 2017

This Fruit of the Spirit maze speaks of the Spirit. There are eight spirits: Kindness, Love, Joy, Goodness, Peace, Patience, Faithfull, and Gentleness. The trees in this maze represent those spirits some have additional branches. The maze begins at the dove in the middle at the bottom you must travel through each of the spirits in the maze to reach the end at the top right corner.

© 2013 Shelly P. Emerson

This Guiding Light maze has to do with God waiting at His throne at the end of the maze. God's Word is the light unto our feet and pathway as we walk through the dark. The maze begins in the middle at the bottom and ends in the middle at the top. There are some scripture needed to go through to get to the end. God's word is the lamp of our pathway in the daily life as we live day to day.

Power In Prayer

This Power In Prayer maze has to do with Moses leading his people from the Egyptians to the promise Land. He showed his faith in God, as the enemy was getting closer. Moses asked for protection and God produced a tornado of fire to stop the enemy. Moses raised his hands asking God to let him and his people cross the Jordan River. Start at the bottom left corner, and end at the top right corner. You need to travel through the scriptures in order to make it to the end of the maze.

© 2013 Shelly P. Emerson

This Ocean of Life maze has to do with Life letting Jesus guide you to the other side. It begins at the bottom left corner below the ocean of life and ends on the upper right corner of Eternal Life. There are two entrances into the ocean of life. One entry is through Worship and the second is through Fellowship. Satan's kingdom is in the upper left corner of this maze. If you get in to Satan's kingdom do not worry, you can get back out through the bible and still get to Eternal Life at the end.

Heavenly Gate

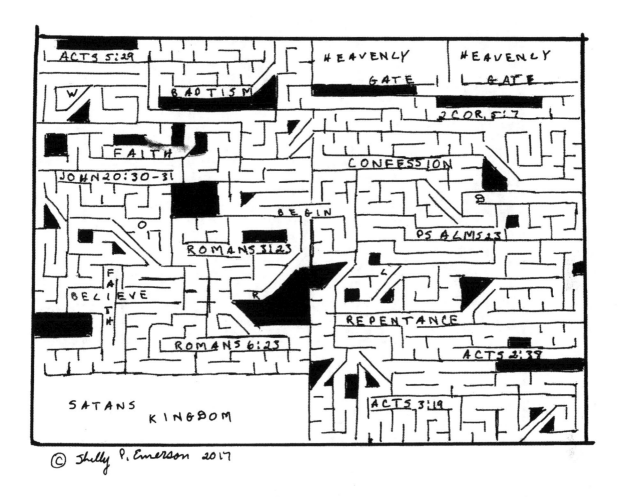

© Shelly P. Emerson 2017

This Heavenly Gate maze is, where we who believe in Jesus the Son of God will meet the saints who are waiting for us. This maze begins in the middle and can end at either the entrance to God's Kingdom at the upper top right corner; or Satan's Evil Kingdom at the lower left corner. There is only one way to enter the gate of Eternal Life

1. Why did Jesus sacrifice His life on the cross?
2. How many days was Jesus dead?
3. What does the resurrection show?

Labels within maze: Baptism, Luke 13:25, Matt 7:7, Repentance, Song 5:2, Acts 2:38, End, Confession, Luke 12:36, Rev. 3:20, Faith, Believe, ST

© 2013 Shelly P. Emerson

This Door maze has to do with Jesus knocking outside the door waiting for your heart to let Him in to your life. The maze begins at the bottom right corner and ends at the door knob where it is locked. The steps to Salvation are in this maze need to be travel through to reach the door knob to let Jesus into your heart

Moses Mountain

© Shelly P. Emerson 2017

This maze Moses' Mountain has to do with Moses' faith in God, Pharaoh put Moses out in the desert he traveled the desert sand, and climbed mountains. The maze begins near the bottom right corner. It ends at the top right, where Moses received water from the women after he protected them from men attacking them and tried taking their flock.

God's Holy Word

© 2013 Shelly P. Emerson

This maze God's Holy Word has to do with contents of God's Word not all of the books are listed; two of the Old Testament and two of the New Testament are. The first book of the bible is Genesis and the last is Revelation of God's Word it contains some scripture. It begins at the top left corner of the open book you must pass through the books that are listed in the maze being that Genesis is the first book and travel through. There is scripture in the maze ends at the bottom right corner. Need to go through the book of Revelation the last book of the bible, to reach the end.

Steps to Salvation

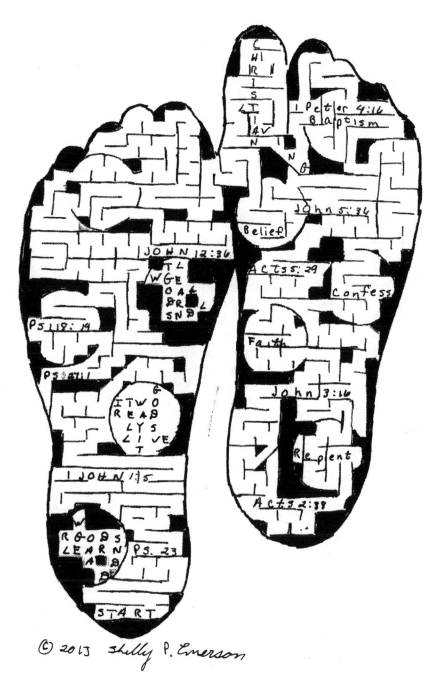

© 2013 Shelly P. Emerson

This maze Steps of Salvation has to do with showing the pathway of salvation as a man walking with Jesus on the beach. The man thought there was only one set of footprints that is when Jesus was carrying him. The maze begins at the bottom left heel and ends at the large right toe at the top of the right foot. Some of the balloons in the left foot print are like word search puzzles. Some show scriptures you must go through the scripture in order to complete the maze. The balloons in the right footprint are the steps to salvation.

© Shelly P. Emerson 2016

The Armor of God maze contains two pieces of armor the shield of faith and the sword of hope they should be worn daily as life goes on. It is used to fight the good fight to eternal life. This maze starts at the bottom right corner and ends at the tip of the sword you need to go through scripture to make to the end.

Fruit of the Spirit

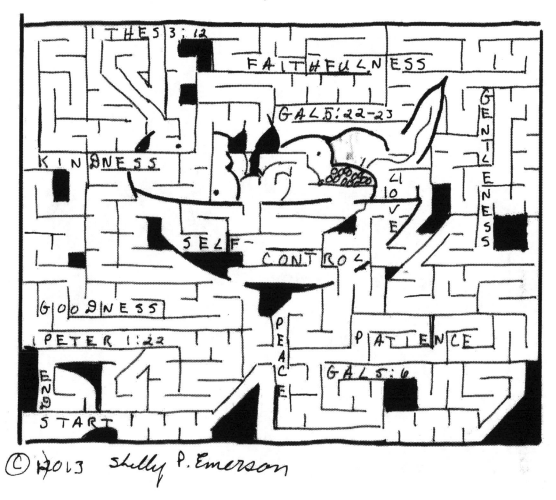

© 2013 Shelly P. Emerson

This Fruit of the Spirit maze contains a list of the Spirit in the bowl of fruit in the middle of the maze. It begins at the bottom left corner and ends above where it started. In order to reach the end, you need to go through each of the spirits names and scriptures. After finished write the names of the spirit below

List of Spirit Fruit

1) _____   5) _____

2) _____   6) _____

3) _____   7) _____

4) _____   8) _____

Jesus' Sacrifice

© 2013 Shelly P. Emerson

This Jesus' Sacrifice maze has to do with the blood Jesus shed on the cross for all our sins; out in society today. It begins at the bottom left corner and ends at the top of the cross where Jesus sacrificed his life for our sins. You must go through the steps of salvation to get to the end.

© 2013 Shelly P. Emerson

This Worldly Life maze has to do with living in this world. There is scripture throughout the maze. It begins in the middle of the globe. You have a choice of ending at either Satan's Kingdom on the bottom left corner of the maze or God's Grace at the top right corner.

© Shelly P. Emerson 2017

The Surviving This World maze has to do with handling things in the world; not letting Satan pull you away from Jesus the Son of God. The maze begins in the middle of the globe and ends at the bottom left corner going through God's Grace on the bottom of the maze.

Spiritual Mind

© 2013 Shelly P. Emerson

This Spiritual Mind maze has to do with having a knowledgeable spirit in this world; and listen to it. It contains things of life that can be used to build a spiritual mind stronger worship, praise, study and read God's word. It begins at the bottom left corner of the maze and ends at the top of the angle's head.

© Shelly P. Emerson 2017

This Key to Salvation maze has to do with giving your life to Jesus, The Son of God. This maze contains the key route to receiving the gift of Eternal Life. The maze begins on the bottom right corner and ends at the top right corner. To make it to the end of the maze, go through each of the keys that represent the path to eternal life in God's Kingdom.

Last Supper

Text visible within the maze image: I COR. 11:23-25, Peter 2:24, MARK 14:22-25, MATTHEW 26:26-29, START

© Shelly P. Emerson 2017

This Last Supper maze is when Jesus had eaten with His disciples before He was beaten and crucified on the cross. He told them what the bread and the cup represented and that He would return in three days. This maze begins on the bottom left corner and ends in the middle of the table at the Last Supper; where the bread of life and cup are on the table.

© Shelly P. Emerson 2017

This maze Excuses of Daily Life shows the number of excuses heard in society daily. Satan is always trying to stop people from giving their life to God, and live for Jesus. The maze begins at the bottom left corner and ends at the front door of the church building in the upper middle of the maze.

This Crazy Maze actually never ends because you can land where you began or next door to where you started; it will land but that is not the end. The theme of this maze is about knowing there is only one God, one Son and one Spirit. It begins in the middle with the choice of four corners, which is also, where it can land on the opposite side of where you started at or land where you start.

© shelly P. Emerson 2017

This maze Mountain of Life has to with climbing the mountain as life goes on and facing challenges in life. Philippians 4:13 says, "I can do all things through Christ who strengthens me." As we live in this world, everyone needs to keep the thought in mind. The maze begins at the bottom near the left and ends at the top right corner. In order to reach the end pass through the scripture and the small word search puzzles inside the maze.

© 2013 Shelly P. Emerson

This Only Through the Cross maze is about receiving the gift of eternal life by giving your life to Jesus. It begins at the bottom left corner and ends at the top right corner In order to get to the end of the maze you must go through each step of salvation scattered in the maze; as you travel the cross. The way to reach the end you must go through each step of Salvation that is scattered in the maze.

© 2013 Shelly P. Emerson

This is a maze of the Old Testament though not all books are listed in this maze you will learn some of the scripture. Going through those books listed in the maze is the only way to reach the end. It begins at the top left corner and you must go through Zechariah to reach the end at the bottom right corner.

My name is Shelly Emerson, I was diagnosed with Epilepsy when I was 5 years old I became a born again Christian in 1975. Because of the Epilepsy, I've become creative with a variety of things. After giving my life to Jesus, I was told by my parents, "The Lord could be using you in some way," I was raised in a Christian environment and taught to stand firm on what I believe. I wrote several stories of experiences I've had throughout my life while attending GED writing, reading, & math classes, continued after I finished GED testing in 2011 and received certificate in 2012. I have no legal issues as to breaking the law or being put in to prison. I'll publish "Life Time Experiences" in the future, I've taken several artistic courses in college and am quite creative in a variety of ways such as greeting cards (holidays, birthday, and sympathy.), book markers; I'll recycle things after cleaning in to use able objects. Enjoy creating mazes & games it has been like therapy to me as to it helps me relax, encourages me to look deeper in to the Bible or American literature. I have visual & verbal multi-intelligence due to the music, sermons, & conversations I hear along with the movies, photos, & landscape I see because ideas of mazes or a craft project will come to mind. The publishing of "Spiritual Mazes & Puzzles" is my first time of publishing a book.

Printed in the United States
by Baker & Taylor Publisher Services